All Kinds of Families

Katie Peters

GRL Consultant Diane Craig,
Certified Literacy Specialist

Pull Ahead READERS

Lerner Publications ◆ Minneapolis

Note from a GRL Consultant
This Pull Ahead leveled book has been carefully designed for beginning readers. A team of guided reading literacy experts has reviewed and leveled the book to ensure readers pull ahead and experience success.

Lerner Publications
An imprint of Lerner Publishing Group, Inc.
241 First Avenue North
Minneapolis, MN 55401 USA

For reading levels and more information, look up this title at www.lernerbooks.com.

Main body text set in Memphis Pro 24/39
Typeface provided by Linotype.

Photo Acknowledgments
The images in this book are used with the permission of: © PeopleImages.com - Yuri A/Shutterstock, p. 3; © NDAB Creativity/Shutterstock, pp. 4–5, 16 (left); © Drazen/Adobe Stock, pp. 6–7, 16 (right); © NDABCREATIVITY/Adobe Stock, pp. 8–9; © imtmphoto/Shutterstock, pp. 10–11, 16 (middle); © Seventyfour/Adobe Stock, pp. 12–13; © IndianFaces/Shutterstock, pp. 14–15.

Front cover: © PeopleImages.com - Yuri A/Shutterstock

Library of Congress Cataloging-in-Publication Data

Names: Peters, Katie author
Title: All kinds of families / written by Katie Peters.
Description: Minneapolis : Lerner Publications, [2026] | Series: Let's look at families | Includes index. | Audience: Ages 4–7 | Audience: Grades K–1 | Summary: "Families come in many sizes. Some have three people; and some have six. Easy-to-read text and engaging photos let beginning readers explore all kinds of families. Pairs with the fiction title, Families in Our Neighborhood"—Provided by publisher.
Identifiers: LCCN 2025011172 (print) | LCCN 2025011173 (ebook) | ISBN 9798765689868 library binding | ISBN 9798348028589 paperback | ISBN 9798765695104 epub
Subjects: LCSH: Families—Juvenile literature | Family size—Juvenile literature
Classification: LCC HQ744 .P393 2026 (print) | LCC HQ744 (ebook) | DDC 306.85—dc23/eng/20250512

LC record available at https://lccn.loc.gov/2025011172
LC ebook record available at https://lccn.loc.gov/2025011173

Manufactured in the United States of America
1 – CG – 12/15/25

All Kinds of Families

Table of Contents

My family has
two people.

My family has
three people.

My family has
four people.

My family has
five people.

My family has
six people.

My family has
many people.

Did You See It?

dad

grandpa

mom

Index